Author's Note:

While physical identities and some details have been changed to protect the vulnerable, this story is based on true events and characters.

Please read with adult supervision.

As a reader, you may find parts of the story confusing and uncomfortable.

I encourage you to save your questions until the end. Your parent, teacher, or facilitator will want to discuss the very things you're thinking about, and they may need a few minutes to turn to the correct set of Discussion Questions for your age, found in the back of this book.

Sincerely,
Wendy Williams

This book is dedicated, with special thanks, to the following people:

-Dan Kittle, Consultant

-Carolyn Sutton, Editorial

-Laura Samano, Back Cover Copy Editorial

-Rose-Hermance Rony, Discussion Questions Editorial

-Jessie Nilo, Illustrator and Designer

-The hundreds of my abolitionist friends out there. You gave me your endorsements, expert advice, and funding to create this weapon against child sex trafficking.

-And of course, to my husband Jason Williams, who prays over this issue and for me every day.

—W.W.

My mother barked and barked at me.

She barked orders,
she barked when I made puddles on the floor,
and she barked when I hadn't done anything at all.

One night I decided I couldn't take her barking anymore.

I ran away to a quiet street corner
where I could cry and be alone.

That is when I met a young girl. She was alone like me.
The girl asked me, "Poor puppy, are you having trouble at home too?"
I tried to whine my story back to her as she bent down to pick me up.

"It's okay," she said. "I am running away too.
We will go together. I will take care of you."

I liked her right away.
She was gentle and shy.
We needed each other.

And she named me "Baby."

One day we met a man.
I wasn't sure I liked him.

He said he would take care of us
and we needed him.

He took us with him.

And he called her "Baby."

For a while, we were very happy together.

He gave us everything we wanted—food and things that made us feel happy and special.

We were just a couple of lucky babies!

But one day, the treats ran out.

The man sent her on car rides that didn't look like fun at all.

He put a chain around my neck, and said I had to wait for her to return with the "bread."

He didn't give any of it to me, though; my bowl was always empty.

Then we were moved from one tiny room to another. It felt worse than living in a dog house.

There was always a chain on the door. I think there must have been a chain on her bed too, for she never left it.

I heard strangers saying my name often.

But I didn't like the sound of it and hid.

And she would cower when they called us "Baby."

We tried to take care of each other, but there was never enough.

Never enough sleep, never enough food, and never enough time off our chains to grow healthy and strong.

We were held together by a chain we couldn't break alone.
We were very sad.

And we cried like babies.

I didn't know how to help her. She didn't know how to help me.
And no longer did they call us "Baby."

One day I pleaded with her to find help. I knew we needed new people.

People who could take care of us.
People who wouldn't hurt us.
People who might show us how to find hope again.

16

We had to say goodbye
to each other.

It hurt to let her go—
but not as much as we had
been hurt already.

She needed help for her.
And I needed help for me.

We bravely grew up a little
that day. No longer
helpless babies.

There, I met a gentle man. I decided to live with him.

I was shy at first.

But he bent down and said, "It's okay Baby, you're going to be happy again."

Then he fed me healthy food that helped me grow big and strong.

I told him my story, with whines and whimpers, and he listened to me patiently.

He cheered me up when I was sad
and taught me how to play.

Now, he takes me on fun car rides to exciting places I have never seen before, like the park!

And best of all, I get lots of wonderful "belly rubs!"

There are no chains keeping he and I together. We are very happy.

We meet nice people and make good friends.

And now I wag my tail and smile when they call me "Baby."

But sometimes at night, while we snuggle in our bed, I dream of her.
I hope she, too, has grown healthy and strong.
I hope she is happy and loved....

Most of all, I hope that like me, she now has only good and kind people to call her "Baby."

If you are in danger, call or text 911.

If someone is keeping you away from other people, threatening you, or forcing you to tell lies, text "help" to 233733.

Discussion Questions

Discussion questions for **grades 3-4** are on pages 24-25.

Discussion questions for **grades 5-8** are on pages 26-27.

Discussion questions for **grades 9+** are on pages 28-29.

See the bottom of page 29 for additional resources.

Grades 3-4 Discussion Questions

1) The story began with Baby having trouble at home.

If you are having trouble understanding why a member of your family behaves as they do . . . talk to an adult you can trust.

• Who are some trusted adults you can talk to?

2) Baby wasn't sure she liked the first man in the story. The man convinced the girl that they needed to go with him.

• Could the man have been a friend of her family?

• Could he have been a community leader, a sports instructor, or a children's program volunteer?

• Could he have been someone she met online?

3) Baby's girl was a victim of **child trafficking.** Child trafficking is the buying, selling, and transportation of children for harmful purposes.

• If you see a kid in your neighborhood that looks hurt, or scared, will you tell someone?

• What treats might the man have promised her to trick her into coming with him?

• Should you go with someone who offers you gifts, fun, or treats?

4) Sometimes we want things that we think will make us happy, but they turn out to not be the best choice.

• Make a list of five wise choices you will make this week that will help you become happy and healthy now and in the future.

1.

2.

3.

4.

5.

5) Baby's girl was a victim of **"bad touch."**

"Bad touch" is any touch that makes a person feel scared or uncomfortable.

• From the story, can you identify at least one time where a "bad touch" occurred?

Grades 3-4 Discussion Questions *(continued)*

6) Baby and her girl were victims of **manipulation**.

Manipulation is when someone tries to force another person to act in a way they do not want to. Manipulation makes people feel guilty, uncomfortable, or afraid.

- **From the story, can you identify at least one time where manipulation was used?**
- **Who used it?**

7) When the mean man sent Baby's girl to get bread, he was not sending her to the grocery store. He was sending her with strangers that paid him money to hurt the girl. The word "bread" was used to hide how they traded money to harm her.

- **Have you ever heard an adult or an older kid use words you don't understand?**
- **What should you do if you hear a word you do not understand that was used in a bad tone?**

8) The story mentioned chains several times, in ways that can be literal or symbolic.

Literal means that there is something real that you can see and touch.

- **Can you find a place in our story in which a literal chain was used?**

[An example of a literal chain in our story is the chain and collar that was used to keep Baby from running away.]

Symbolic is the use of an object, word, picture, or color that represents our feelings. An example is a red heart to represent the way we love our family.

- **Do you think the chains mentioned on pages 8, 9, and 10 are literal or symbolic?**

[An example of a symbolic chain in our story may include the junk food, phone, stimulants, or things used to manipulate and control the habits of the young girl.]

9) Baby and the girl now have a whole new life.

- **Do you think the girl in our story is happy in her new life?**
- **Why, or why not?**

Grades 5-8 Discussion Questions

The story contains examples of three types of child abuse: **Neglect, physical, and emotional abuse.**

1) **Neglect** is a form of abuse that includes the failure of an adult to provide food, weather-appropriate clothing, a safe environment, medical attention, emotional support, and love.

- Can you identify a time Baby or the girl experienced neglect?

- What might be some signs of neglect you can watch for with your friends and neighbors??

[Examples: frequent absences from school, signs of being excessively hungry, poor hygiene practices, begging or stealing money, needing medical care, someone who has witnessed drug or alcohol activity in the home, or lack of supervision.]

2) **Physical abuse** includes "bad touch" [defined on page 24], being hit or beaten, being starved by someone on purpose, indecent exposure, forced sexual acts, or anything intending to cause physical harm.

- Can you identify a time that Baby or the girl experienced physical abuse?

- What might be some signs of physical abuse you can watch out for with your friends and neighbors?

[Examples: unexplained bruises, broken bones, black eyes, burns on skin, showing fear, over-compliance, excessive aggression, or constant mood changes.]

3) **Emotional abuse** includes yelling, blaming, threatening, bullying, and belittling a person.

- Can you identify a time that Baby or the girl experienced emotional abuse?

- What might be some signs of emotional abuse you can watch out for with your friends and neighbors?

[Examples: self-isolating behavior, extreme aggression, passiveness, not caring about anything, threatening, bullying, or suicidal tendencies.]

4) In the story, Baby did not trust the first man. However, Baby didn't listen to her instincts; instead, she went with the man, because the girl decided to trust him.

- What would you do if someone made you feel uncomfortable or uneasy?

- What if you're not sure *why* you feel uncomfortable? What then?

5) Baby felt alone at certain points in the story.

- When is it okay to be alone?

- When is it NOT okay to be alone?

Grades 5-8 Discussion Questions *(continued)*

6) Make a list together.

- **What are some good characteristics that build a healthy friendship/relationship between two people?**

- **What are some characteristics that could contribute to a harmful friendship/relationship?**

Good Relationships	Harmful Relationships

7) Baby's girl was a victim of **child sex trafficking.**

Child sex trafficking is the buying, selling, and transportation of children for the purpose of sexual acts.

- **If you see a kid in your neighborhood who looks hurt or scared, will you tell someone?**

- **Do you think teenagers are more likely to be abducted on the street, or to be enticed by a new friend who offers gifts, money, adventures, and special treats?**

8) In the story, the first man that Baby and the girl meet appears to want to help them, but after gaining their trust, he uses their new friendship to manipulate and hurt them.

This act of preparing a child to be trafficked is called **grooming.** People make money by grooming a child to be sold. A **child groomer** can be any age, race, or gender.

- **In the story, what were some things the trafficker used to "groom" Baby and the girl?**

- **What might be some signs you should watch for in your relationships to avoid being "groomed?"**

[Examples: excessive compliments, gifts, presenting themselves as the only person who understands, asking you to keep secrets from your parents, offering favors like extra help with sports or homework in an isolated setting, and especially non-age-appropriate online conversations and relationships]

Grades 9 and up Discussion Questions

1) There are at least three occurrences of abuse that took place in the story. [Types of abuse defined on page 26.]

- **Can you identify all three types of abuse?**

2) Baby's girl was a victim of child sex trafficking.

Child Sex Trafficking is the buying, selling, and transporting of children for commercial sex acts. It takes place through the use of force, deception, or coercion.

- **If you see a child in your neighborhood who looks hurt or scared, will you tell someone?**

- **Will you call 911, or will you report it to an adult?**

- **Can you think of any other reporting options that may fall in between the above two options?**

3) Baby and her girl were victims of **grooming.**

Child grooming is the process by which a predator gains the trust of a child or teenager to take advantage of them for sexual purposes.

This grooming process involves the following methods:
a) Targeting the victim
b) Gaining the victim's trust
c) Filling a need in the victim's life
d) Isolating the victim
e) Sexualizing the relationship
f) Maintaining control of the victim

- **Can you think of one part in the story where you see signs of the victim being groomed?**

- **Are only young girls victims of grooming?**

Predators use online chats, apps, games, and social media with the intent of targeting and grooming victims.

- **What are some ways you can protect yourself, your friends, and your siblings from becoming victims of grooming?**

[Examples: Attend an anti-trafficking meeting in your area to learn more about the current risks in your community. Avoid gaming with those you don't know. Never enter private chat forums or private in-person meetings. Join a community mentorship program in which you can be a positive influence in another's life. Consider a monitoring app that detects clues in language, pictures, and a predator's patterns on any electronic device.]

4) Grooming, abuse, and trafficking often go unreported because victims and even witnesses have been taught to fear authority figures.

- **What if you suspect your best friend is at-risk of being groomed, who could you contact?**

- **Now, what if you noticed something that seemed "off" in someone you don't know? Would you report it to a school counselor, or a trusted adult? Do you need to find another friend first in order to discuss your "off" feeling?**

- **Should you keep your feelings to yourself and ignore them because you have no "proof"?**

- **Would you want someone to do the same for you? Why or why not?** [Also: See "More Resources", p. 29.]

Grades 9 and up Discussion Questions *(continued)*

5) If your mood, happiness, and identity are being defined by and dependent on another person, you could be in a **codependent relationship.**

Codependence is [but is not limited to]:

The inability to be alone

Obsessive fear of abandonment

Controlling or being controlled

A feeling of deep responsibility for the happiness of others

Compromising your personal boundaries

- **What types of things might someone say or do to pull another person into a codependent relationship?**

- **If you have questions about a relationship in your life, who are some trusted adults you should confide in?**

5) There are contradicting beliefs about the differences and similarities of prostitution and sex trafficking. These varying opinions affect the authority of law enforcement every day.

- **In a short essay, can you research and highlight the differences and similarities?**

6) Did you know that child victims of sex trafficking who turn 18 are often convicted of prostitution while their trafficker roams free? One reason is that the trauma of human trafficking is so great that many victims are too overwhelmed to seek help, even if the resources are readily available, or to report their predator because of fear. The girl in Baby's story exhibited bravery, just by seeking help.

- **What are some ways for the community, law enforcement, and you to help victims of trafficking?**

- **In your opinion, where do you think the girl in Baby's story is now?**

More Resources

If you or someone else is being trafficked, text "Help" to **233733**. For more information, text "Info" to **233733**.

If you suspect someone is a victim of human trafficking or needs help connecting with a service provider in your area, or to learn more, contact the National Human Trafficking Hotline: **1-888-373-7888**

To report **suspected abuse** of any kind, please contact your local Child Protective Services immediately.

To report a missing or exploited child, contact the National Center for Missing or Exploited Children: **1-800-843-5678**

Perk your ears up for the language of trafficking. For a Glossary of Sex Trafficking Terms, visit **inpublicsafety.com**

To take protective steps to guard your child against online cyber grooming, visit **www.bark.us**